GLENN MURCUTT

University of Washington Master Studios and Lectures

Distributed by the

University of Washington Press

PO Box 50096

Seattle, WA 98145-5096

www.washington.edu/uwpress

Library of Congress Cataloging-in-Publication Data

Murcutt, Glenn.

Glenn Murcutt : University of Washington master studios and lectures / edited by Jim Nicholls. — 1st ed.

    p. cm.

ISBN 978-0-295-98958-7 (pbk. : alk. paper)

1. Murcutt, Glenn. 2. Architecture—Philosophy. 3. University of

Washington. Dept. of Architecture. 4. Architecture—Study and teaching

(Graduate)—Washington—Seattle. I. Nicholls, Jim, 1958– II. Title. III.

Title: University of Washington master studios and lectures.

NA1605.M87A35 2009

720.92—dc22   2009015878

The paper used in this publication meets the minimum requirements of American National Standard for Information Sciences—Permanence of Paper for Printed Library Materials, ANSI Z39.48–1984.

Front cover: Glenn Murcutt sketch from exchanges with students in the 2008 studio

Back cover: Photo of Glenn Murcutt by Jim Nicholls

GLENN MURCUTT

University of Washington Master Studios and Lectures

Edited by Jim Nicholls

Department of Architecture, University of Washington

CONTENTS

OBSERVATION AND EXCHANGE

Jim Nicholls

Todd Coglon + Glenn Murcutt in UW studio

Photo: Peter Cohan

Australian Architect Glenn Murcutt led Master Studios at The University of Washington Department of Architecture for five years beginning in 2004. Each year Glenn came twice a quarter for over two weeks of daily exchanges. Every afternoon was for talking and drawing with students, evenings were often spent giving well-attended public lectures, and dinner was shared with students, professors and practitioners.

Spending time with Glenn was an education. Each encounter an exchange of observation and information – anecdotal, informal, but intense and acute. Taken together a set of rigorous principles emerged.

To convey this experience it is necessary to provide a sense of the exchange, to hear Glenn's voice as he engages with his students and his audience. An accurate representation must capture the passionate excitement, and the didactic clarity.

Glenn's teaching builds up from accumulated experiences. It does not attempt to reduce active principles to static rules, or privilege the discourse of a particular moment. By layering discrete descriptions within this book, a composite portrait of clear and articulate lessons emerges and informs.

This text presents that portrait with edited excerpts from Glenn Murcutt's lectures, dialogues, and students' projects from the Master Studios. Additionally, UW teaching colleagues provide notes about their own experiences with Glenn and his students.

End

GLENN TIME

Peter Cohan

Every day is a studio day when Glenn is in town - Saturdays, Sundays and holidays. For each Master Studio he makes two trips to Seattle, lasting eight and seven days respectively, typically during the third and seventh weeks of the ten-week quarter. Students suspend all other activities in order to focus exclusively on studio during these visits.

Glenn's first teaching day always includes a site visit and a presentation by the students of the site analysis that was conducted during the weeks prior. The importance of understanding the subtle nuances of site becomes clear as Glenn peppers the students with questions about climate, habitat, vegetation, geology, and topography.

The remainder of the week is devoted to design process. A table in the center of studio becomes the focus of activity. Studio begins at noon each day. One by one the students spread their drawings on the table and a three-way conversation ensues between student, Murcutt and the regular studio instructor. Glenn, pencil in hand, leads the session, using exploratory sketching, relevant anecdotes and directed questions to draw surprising insights from the students. Extra chairs around the table provide an opportunity for students from other studios to sit in on these sessions. Glenn leaves only after everyone has had a half hour turn. When he leaves, the studio turns its attention to producing new drawings and study models for the following day.

On the last day of Glenn's first visit students present their schematic designs to their invited critics from the college. The tone of the review is positive; however, Glenn makes very clear the improvements

Glenn leaving the Simpson-Lee house, Mt. Wilson,
NSW, Australia
Photo: Rick Mohler

he expects to see in each project by the time of his next visit.

During the interim between visits, students continue to refine their projects under the tutelage of the regular studio instructor. This exploratory development includes the construction of 1/2" scale section models, which become the focus of the first day of Glenn's second visit.

Upon his return the studio reverts to "Glenn time" again; however, there is a shift in focus from issues of site and building to those of building and detail. Details that respond to sunlight, wind and rain, that acknowledge the expansion, contraction and weathering of materials, that are honest, elegant and appropriate, are coaxed out of the students during that final week. Students labor right up to the day of the final review. There will be time to produce final presentation-quality drawings and models during the weeks that follow Glenn's departure.

The review on Glenn's last day celebrates the results of this intensive studio experience. Reviewers are chosen from the many friends Glenn has made over a lifetime of teaching and lecturing around the world. He typically lets his distinguished colleagues have their say about each project first, before adding his own observations and summing up. After the review a "barbie" behind the school, attended by current and former students, reviewers, and faculty provides an appropriate send-off for Glenn before he returns to Australia the following day.

End

ENVIRONMENTAL RESEARCH & LEARNING CENTER

Shaw Island, Washington
Glenn Murcutt + Peter Cohan | 2004

CLASS LIST - Evan Bourquard, Katie Cox, Kate Cudney, Maria Do, Sean Kakigi, Laura Lenss, Ed Rossier, Andres Villaveces, Matt Wallace, Mark Ward, Sara Wise

The Cedar Rock Biological Preserve, given to the University of Washington as a gift from Robert H. Ellis, Jr., is dedicated for use as a natural preserve for scientific and educational research and for promoting the values of natural environments. With an increased urgency towards the restoration, documentation and preservation of the 370 acres that comprise the reserve, it has become apparent that there is a substantial need for the construction of a research and learning center on the preserve. The center will house up to six full-time researchers and will also have space for groups of students who will be directly involved with preservation and rehabilitation. The research staff will be required to stay a minimum of three-months, while student groups will be encouraged to stay a minimum of one week on site. These requirements will help to reduce the physical impact on the site, and give the residents a greater connection to the Shaw Island community as well as to the preserve.

PROGRAM

Research: Research Laboratory/Workroom, Private Offices (3), Storage/ Equipment Room, Cleaning and Drying Area, Herbarium

Teaching/Learning: Large Meeting Room, Outreach Education (optional), Computer Support

Living: Long Term Faculty Sleeping Rooms (3), Short Term Sleeping Rooms (for 16), Kitchen, Bath (2), Tent Platform (optional)

Support Services: Mechanical, General Rest Room, Laundry, Vehicle/ Tool Storage

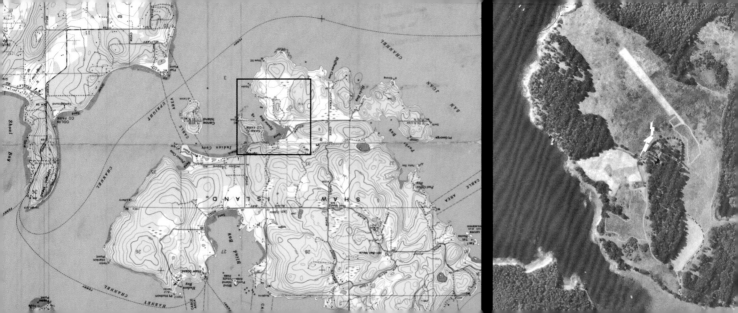

CONVERSATION WITH STUDENTS

Glenn Murcutt

April 12, 2004

Katie Cox, 2004

Left | Building Model

Student: I have a question about how do you go about creating a relationship with the builders? Getting the kind of quality... [inaudible]

Glenn Murcutt: Yes, that's a really good question, actually. You know, I was raised in the era where architects and builders were different breeds. And an architect would come on the site, and if the work wasn't good enough, the architect would say either, 'Not good enough,' or 'Come,' and just push the wall over and say, 'This is shocking work.' Now, this is not a way to satisfy people's inner self-esteem.

S: (laughter)

GM: And I intuitively worked another way. And it wasn't till I was made aware of it by a builder that I became conscious of doing it and making sure I did what I was doing on every job. And what it amounted to was this: Because the jobs were often located in fair distant places, I would arrive either at morning teatime or arrive at lunchtime. And I was thirsty and I'd just automatically ask, 'Look, you guys, I need a cuppa tea. What about getting me a cuppa tea?' Well, they were shocked. That an architect should ask them to sit down, and sit down with the builders and ask for a cuppa tea. And then they'd start to offer me a sandwich, and I said, 'Yeah, give me a sandwich.' And all of a sudden, they couldn't believe that I was just doing this.

And I know that if you go and see a bad piece of workmanship, [inaudible] just directly to that person say, 'That's not good enough.' It's hurtful. I understand it's hurtful. So what I'd do, is when I saw something really bad, I wouldn't say a thing. This was innate, what I did initially. And I would go

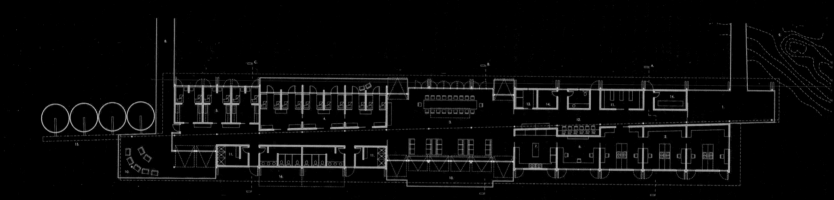

round, and I would look to see where that same trades person had done it really well. And I'd call the foreman over. And I'd say to the foreman, 'You know, who's responsible for this work?' And he'd say, 'Oh, Bill Blundell's done that thing, the welder.' I said, 'It's absolutely fantastic work. Fantastic.' And of course the foreman's pride'd go up, and he'd get one of his men, and he'd call Bill over and say, 'Bill, the architect's just said this is fantastic work.' And Bill's pride'd go up, and he'd think this was wonderful that-' And I said, 'Look, if you can get that standard of work, I'd say, get this standard of work, you'll have a very happy architect at the end of this process.' Well, this guy was eating out of my hand.

S: (laughter)

GM: And you'd then go around the job a half-hour later, come up to this really shit house stuff and say, 'Hey, Bill, look at this.' And he'd say, 'Whoo, not good, is it?' I said, 'No, it'd be great if you could fix it.' He said, 'Oh sure, sure. Get it fixed.' This happens every time. Without exception. Not an argument. If you go to him, and go there first, he's lost self-esteem, lost pride, feels terrible, he feels absolutely pushed down. It's the worst thing you can do to any human. You've gotta find the things that have been addressed very well. That is extremely important. Once you've done that, and you show what good work they can do, and they can show you, then you can develop a relationship with those trades-people on that job.

Now, I learned about it because my builder, a Finnish builder – and I have many builders I've worked with-I must've worked with perhaps fifty or sixty builders in my career. But one particular builder, a Finn, two guys, Lasse Kaukkauma and Yokoberg, both are fantastic builders. And yet their sub-trades, sometimes, were not quite as good. But they were the ones that first appreciated my sitting down and having morning tea with them. And then got such confidence in our relationship that they said, 'Why don't you come and join us for a sauna?' Well, there's nothing like a sauna to bring the raw truth out of everything. And I'd go down on a Friday night, and have a few stiff vodkas and there were a couple of occasions where I couldn't drive home; I didn't drive home. With some Finnish sausage, which is enough to kill you...

S: (laughter)

GM: ...together with the vodka, and they came out with all these wonderful relationship stories.

Evan Bourquard, 2004

Left | Building plan

15

They said to me, 'You know, it is such a privilege to be building your work. Because you really appreciate what we're doing. And you let us know.' And that's what the important thing is, to let them know. And they said, 'For you to come down and sit... you're the only architect we've worked with,' and Lasse Kaukkama, he was about sixty at the time, said, 'In my forty years in working as a builder, you're the only one that's come and sat down with us.' And he said, 'Furthermore, you can go on the job Monday morning and say to us that it's not good enough, and we accept that, because you're right.'

On my very first morning on the first job I had designed, they won the tender for it. I hadn't know of them at all before. I'd heard about them. Lasse Kaukkauma, the senior member who was about fifty-five at the time, he had all these Finnish guys, all these tradesmen. And one Finnish woman who was a painter with her husband. And he lined every one of them up. And he took me down the line and shook hands, and introduced me to every one of them in this line, and they all had their hats, and they took them off to me, and nodded their heads, and shook hands, and it went from that.

And today, the last building that was completed is my own house. It's the last building. Kaukkauma died four years ago, and Berger's retired as from my last building. Whether I've punished him so much that he says 'No more,' I'll soon find out. But it has been a very rewarding time in the way I've got perhaps eight or nine builders in the state of New South Wales, and I've got one is south Australia, and I've got one in Victoria, fantastic builders. I have a fantastic relationship with them. I can go out with them, I can enjoy their company, I can be a fried with them, and I can also say to them that it's not good enough without being offensive. Does that answer your question? Any other questions?

S: Most people know about how you are very regional, well, within your country of Australia. So I'm wondering if that was a conscious decision, or is it just something that came about, knowing your homeland and eventually developing all your work there?

GM: Yeah. Um, well, most of you will have heard that I am a sole practitioner... and I practice in a very private, small way. And because I don't employ people, I don't practice outside Australia. But the principles I tried to work with in Australia are about questions. And those questions are internationally transferable. It's very simple-Where does the sun come from? Where does the wind come from?

"Because my father was, as I said, a very good designer, and design to him was a response to where you were."

Where does the bad weather come from? Where does the good weather come from? When does it come? When doesn't it come? What is a snowfall, what is the cold, icy weather, what is the topography, what is the hydrology, what is the geothermology? What is the geography, what are the plants, what is the flora, what's the fauna? What's the history? What's the ancient history of the land... right through the American Indian history, right through history, right through to the current time. Those questions I ask of my own land, as I would be able to transfer to here. And the regional side of my work really comes through my family. Because my father was, as I said, a very good designer, and design to him was a response to where you were.

So the regional response that I've been most interested in is- I've been greatly involved with landscape. I love landscape. If I wasn't an architect, I'd be a landscape architect. I just think landscape architecture is fantastic. I think plants, flora... just the most wondrous elements in our daily life. What a privilege it is to see the beauty of landscape. To go up to your north Cascades, to go to the south Cascades ...to go to Mount Rainier...

S: Glenn, I have a question. In your Alderten House, it was designed and built not only for a family, but for the community as well?

GM: Yeah.

S: Um, do you that think this type of gesture, opening your home to the community, is something that we need to be looking at more, in terms of incorporating into the residential, and if so, how?

GM: Well, let me qualify that. Aboriginal people don't own land. They have never owned land. The land is their mother. You don't possess your mother. The land is your mother, which is the gift of life. You respect it as you respect your mother. You respect it as the gift of life. So there's no such thing as a knowledge of subdivision. There's no such thing a a community possession. But there is a land right of occupancy. So if your culture is historically related to that area of land, for anybody else to come onto that land, is to intrude.

So I suggest that, first of all, it's a community house because the land is community land.

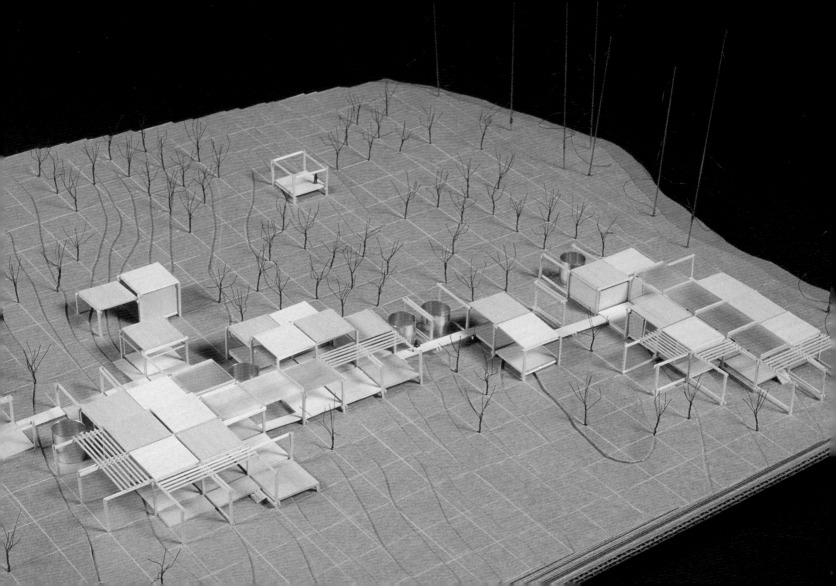

Laura Lenss, 2004

Left | Site Model

Above Left | Tectonic Model

Above Right | Tectonic Model Detail

And therefore the house is community house, equally, that you don't possess the materials of your house; they've been gifted. You don't catch animals in the Aboriginal world; the animals gift themselves. An entirely different concept. In Aboriginal world, they look at us, and laugh at us and say that 'You all work on the basis of survival of the fittest. We're the longest living culture on this planet, we represent survival of cooperation.' Entirely different concept of living. So their survival is through cooperation.

And my client, the one you referred to, Rika House, Bunduck was a very good friend of Jenny's and she had lived in Jenny's house for long periods. And she happened to be one of the speakers at these seminars, and she was told I was there in the audience. So she came up to me and she said that she had lived in Jenny's house, and that if you're gonna live in a white fellow's place, Jenny's house was good enough for a black fellow. Exactly her words. And I asked her why. She said it was a healthy building. And I said, 'What do you mean a healthy building?' She said, as an Aboriginal person, we need to see the horizon. We need to see the daily climatic changes. We need to see who's coming and who's going. The horizon tells us the weather pattern changes. The horizon tells us who's coming and who's going, and the horizon tells us what animals are passing and coming and going. And she said, 'I need to be able to look out from in the access way that I'm moving along to see these things.

Continued on page 25

NISQUALLY ENVIRONMENTAL EDUCATION CENTER

Nisqually National Wildlife Refuge, Washington
Glenn Murcutt + Peter Cohan | 2005

CLASS LIST - Carl Baker, Travis Bell, Morgan Ennis, Karen Esswein, Brad Gassman, Kristina Kessler, Scott Kuchta, Carly Mendelssohn, Jeff Ottem, Chad Robertson, Lauren Tindall, Ian Withers

The Nisqually River Delta, a biologically rich and diverse area at the southern end of Puget Sound, supports a variety of habitats. Here, the freshwater of the Nisqually River combines with the saltwater of Puget Sound to form an estuary rich in nutrients and detritus. Three thousand acres of salt and freshwater marshes, grasslands, riparian, and mixed forest habitats provide resting and nesting areas for migratory waterfowl, songbirds, raptors, and wading birds.

Each year approximately 5,000 students, teachers, and group leaders visit the Nisqually National Wildlife Refuge It offers an invaluable opportunity for students to experience and learn about the natural world.

The Final Comprehensive Conservation Plan and Environmental Impact Statement for Nisqually National Wildlife Refuge was released in late August 2004. It calls for expansion of the environmental education program so that it can serve up to 15,000 students annually. The primary users will be class groups, from kindergarten through high school, and other youth organizations from around the Puget Sound. The facility will occasionally be open to the general public for special events, such as the Nisqually Watershed Festival.

PROGRAM

Welcoming: Lobby/Entrance/Mudroom, Orientation Area, Office

Teaching/Learning:

Classroom A: Wildlife and Habitat

Classroom B: People, Land and Water

Viewing Deck

Support Services: Kitchenette, Rest Rooms, Storage, Janitor's Closet, Mechanical Room

Carl Baker, 2005

Left | Site Model

Above | Site Section

I also need to be able to open and close the building. That I don't feel like I want to kick the walls out. That I can actually see and feel and feel the climate from inside-what's happening outside.' She said, 'This is the start of healthy buildings.'

S: (laughter)

GM: So I'm interested in aspiration. That's really important. That's a wonderful aspect of humans, to aspire to something really wonderful. To aspire to do something really important. To aspire to do something very responsible.

End

"I tell my students: you must put into your work first effort,
second love, and third suffering."

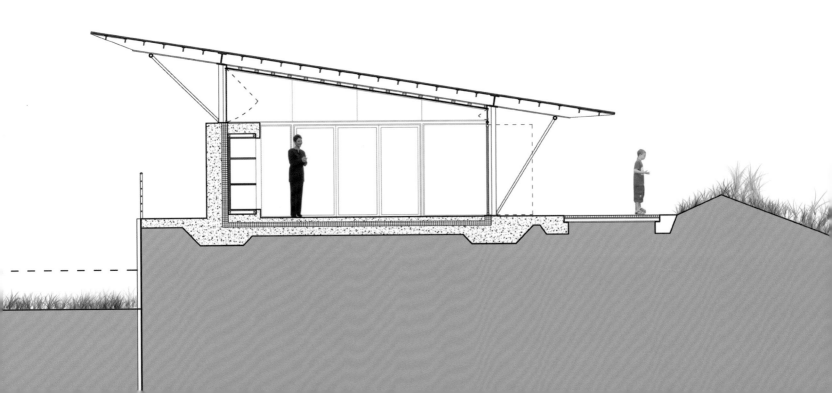

CALLISON NOON-HOUR LECTURE

Glenn Murcutt
May 17, 2007

Scott Kuchta, 2005

Left | Building Section

27:05

Glenn Murcutt: ...my father used to say to me as one of the principles of going into practice, son, never be in a rush to be a success and I think he was probably pretty right. I've taken a long time to get into doing public buildings.

28:11

...[he also] said: 'Always realize that you've got to go further than you think you can go... and I think that's a really important thing to remember, particularly for young architects. I think it's a really important thing to remember that it does take time to develop architecture. It takes time to do architecture. Architecture is not one of those things that you can do, just flash it out, overnight. I gave a lecture here last year that Steve was just talking to me about that he appreciated, where I showed how with the development of an idea you go forwards two steps and you come back one step. You might go back three steps, then... the two steps forward you made are not lost because you jump over that again, because you found another direction, or a better way of doing it, or a more economic way, a more poetic way. Very often the poetics and the rational together, when they combine, the building starts to sing. And I think it's a very important stage in any work of architecture.

So, as [Jose Coderch] said to me, and I might have quoted this last year, but I quote it to all the students, he said, 'I tell my students: you must put into your work first effort, second love, and third suffering.' And let me assure you, if you don't suffer in this profession, there's something wrong.

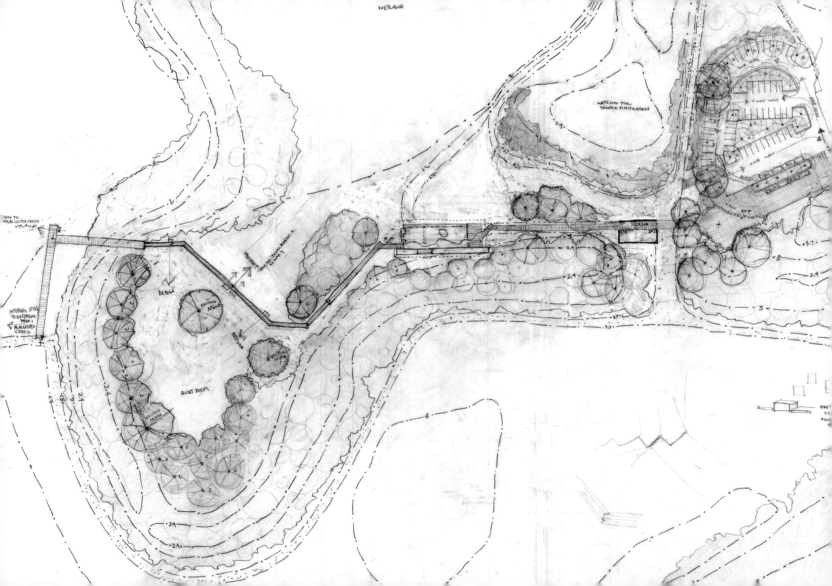

WETLAND

WETLAND FOR
SEWAGE PURIFICATION

GUEST ROOM

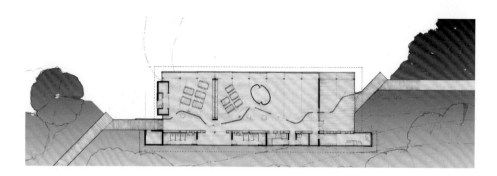

Karen Esswein, 2005

Left | Site Plan

Above | Building Plan

[Audience laughter]

And he said to me, and of course it's very Catholic, Spanish Catholic, as well, but it's a reality also, and he said, 'Even if the work is not great, it will show that care and dedication.' I think he was right.

He also said to me, 'with every new building, I am very nervous.' And you know, no architect ever told me, he or she was nervous before they got started to work on a new building. They all seemed to be terribly confident to me. Getting it to work. Floor-space ratio. Got that solved. Number of floors? Yeah, got all that sorted out. Side cover right, done, done. Up Thirty-five floors. We're right. We're there. What's the façade about? What's this about? What's that about? You know, I think that [sigh] architecture, can be very deep, and it can have a huge number of layers. And the anxiety that [Kedirk] told me about released me, as a human, as well as an architect, because I was almost frozen to the point of inactiveness. I just couldn't progress any further; I was so frightened. And to know that it's perfectly okay to be frightened, in fact it's a necessary component to be frightened, not that it's just alright, was a very, very, very great release for me. And I think they're some of the issues that are before all of us. The idea of just being confident in itself is important: having the confidence to know that you'll find a result, but the anxiety to know that you don't know how you're going to get there. And the greatest ability an architect can have, in my view, is to know when it's still not good enough. And I think that's a really important ability: to know that it's still not good enough. That is a critical ability.

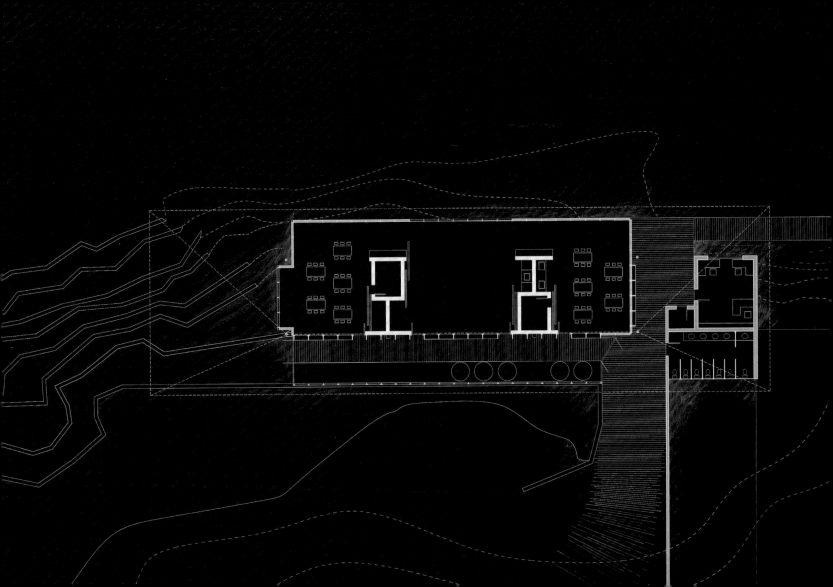

"And whilst I drive the students extraordinarily hard, I do it because I drive myself hard. As an architect, I drive myself very hard."

34:52

And whilst I drive the students extraordinarily hard, I do it because I drive myself hard. As an architect, I drive myself very hard. I'm now over seventy, and I still have enthusiasm of a of a thirty year old, probably some greater enthusiasm than many thirty year olds...

    As I tell the students, 'Never be afraid of losing a good idea because there are so many other good ideas. All you have to do is discover them.' I don't believe in the act as-such of creativity in itself; I believe that there's a process of creativity, but the act is one of discovery. Our role as architects is that of the discoverer. Any work of architecture that exists, any work of architecture that has the potential to exist, is there to be discovered, not there to be created, in my view. It's nothing to do with creation. I think it's a matter of discovery. It's a path to discovery, and the path to discovery is the process that's creative, it's the way you go about that discovery that is very important to me.

37:00

[Glenn begins to draw on board]

47:36

...uh. And we can look into that tunnel to really experience the quality of being in a genuine mine, not a fake one. And so it is, architecture is about the experience. It's about, as I said before, the 'ings' of things. The arriving, the smelling, the perceiving, the touching, the caring, ...all those things of looking, arriving, walking, viewing, it is those 'ings' that I think are the essence of much of architecture.

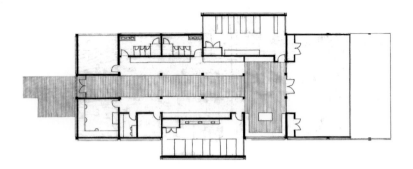

Lauren Tindall, 2005

Left | Interior Rendering

Above | Building Plan

54:26

You can regulate the air flow as well as the moisture level that's in there and the level of cooling independent of all, it modifies the velocity outside there. So, [sigh] it's a really nice sort of way of working in my view. It's related to understanding light and heat and ...evaporation for the cooling process. It's related to positive pressures, negative pressures, how air moves. They're paths, they're all to do with paths, there's the: path of air, the path of water, the path of recirculation, the paths of collection. We collect all the water from coming off these roofs here, they all flow into gutters that come down into a huge storage area down underneath the building in here, so we've got cold water throughout the year which you can't get anywhere else in town. So we're - these are all the paths that we're dealing with. And I think they're the sum of things that aren't dealt with often.

56:18

So you get these regimes that are about the water...

56:47

...and then on top of that you've got altitude and latitude. All these sorts of things start to bring in the differences that are occur in our landscape. Then you've got your soil conditions. Then you have your climatic conditions, and the heat and the sun. These all make differences to the measurement of place and what occurs in place. But we also possess it on our bodies, from our forehead to our eyebrow to

Continued on page 37

KENMORE AIR TERMINAL

Seattle, Washington
Glenn Murcutt + Rick Mohler | 2006

CLASS LIST - Todd Beyreuther, Rebecca Cook, Emily Doe, Blake Gallagher, Greg Hale, Emma Nowinski, Kozo Nozawa, Erik Perka, Rebecca Roberts, Adam Shick, Brett Smith, Monica Willemsen

The project consists of a new float plane terminal and exhibition space for Kenmore Air on the southwest corner of Lake Union in Seattle. Kenmore Air is the world's second largest float plane airline and an essential part of Seattle's history and identity. The project affords the opportunity to explore a building at the intersection of land, water and air that will act as a threshold between Seattle and the region beyond. The exhibition component will be dedicated to the display and history of float planes, which were essential to the development of Seattle and aviation.

Kenmore Air currently serves an estimated 70,000 customers per year from the south Lake Union terminal. During the peak season (April to September) surge conditions occur throughout the terminal resulting in a lack of seating and efficient passenger circulation.

The site is between Westlake Ave N and the Lake Union shoreline. It is adjacent to South Lake Union Park and is within view of the Center for Wooden Boats to the southeast and Seattle Center to the southwest. The adjacent South Lake Union neighborhood is in a state of accelerated change as numerous mixed-use building projects are currently being planned or under construction.

PROGRAM

Terminal: Check-In, Lounge, Arrival/Departure Gate, US Customs

Administrative: Staff Office, Pilot Prep, Break Room

Public Spaces: Entry/Lobby, Exhibition, Café/Gift Shop, Observation Deck

Support Services: Rest Rooms, Storage, Janitor's Closet, Mechanical Room, Telecommunications Room, Loading Dock

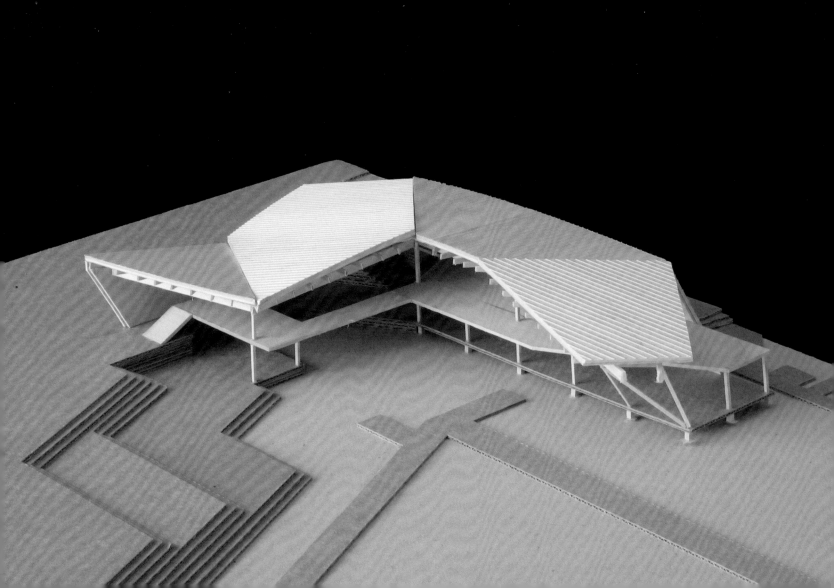

Brett Smith, 2006

Left | Preliminary Model, seen from above

Above | Final Model, seen from water

our eyelid to our eyelash to our eye. There are all these zones that are working all the time, and they're the edges, they're all the edges of things. And something that we've almost forgotten about is what edges mean. And edges to buildings are important. Most of my buildings are breathing at the edges. They're perceiving the edges.

I refer to the buildings as, in many ways, not designing a building but designing, in a sense... that is, that buildings are designed in a way [like] musical instruments, [which] I am sure were never designed to say, 'This is again going to be a beautiful object.'

The violin, the cello, any of the brass instruments. They haven't been designed to be beautiful things in themselves. They come out of an understanding of what their performance is to be. And when you think of a score of music that's written by an incredible mind, that's performed by one person to an orchestra, that is perceived by the audience that are there listening to the sound; they're listening to the mind of the original composer passing through all these instruments. I think architecture's not that much different.

I think the building is not necessarily an object. A lot of people have seen my buildings as 'objects in the landscape.' They're not simply objects in the landscape. We are the receptors. We live in these buildings. So these buildings capture the winter sunlight, they exclude the summer sunlight. So they're performing as an instrument. They pick up the winds that are coming in the summer, the north-east breezes off the coast. And you can smell the sea salt in it, or in summertime you put your flowering

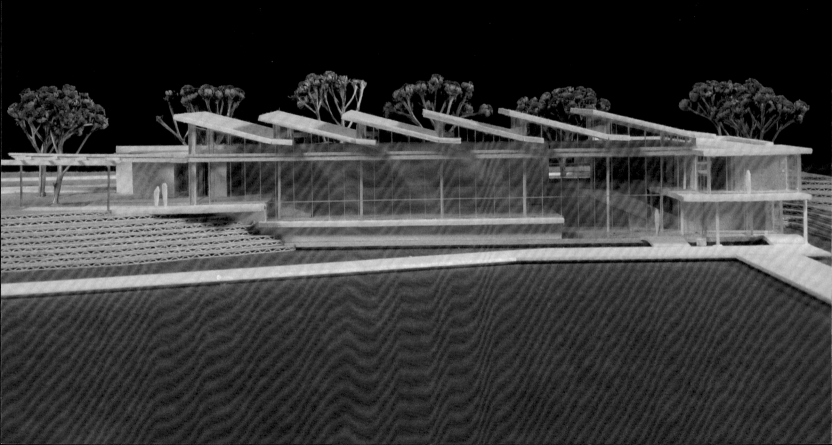

"...so the building becomes in a sense the instrument to all these things around us that are being picked up and being translated for you, as the participant, to experience."

Eric Perka, 2006

Left | Building Model, East Facade

plants that perfume to your north-east. Pick up the perfumes, you can smell it coming into the house. It's very important.

59:50

...so the building becomes in a sense the instrument to all these things around us that are being picked up and being translated for you, as the participant, to experience.

1:00:54

...and I think that's where I feel very comfortable in my world of dealing with architecture as a modifier of our elements.

1:02:54

Audience Member: You've obviously been involved with a lot of students from the early parts of your career... So I've got two questions for you: 1. What advice do you give people early in their careers to help them perpetuate and be successful? 2. And what advice would you give those of us who have been around for a while on how to help?

GM: Well the two of you should get to be the first to start (gestures towards the partners of Callison) [Audience laughter]

GM: Listening is the most important thing. Be able to listen, understand, and then make a judgment. I'll quote some of my father's things. When I was going into practice, and this was shortly before his death, I said to him, I was going into practice.

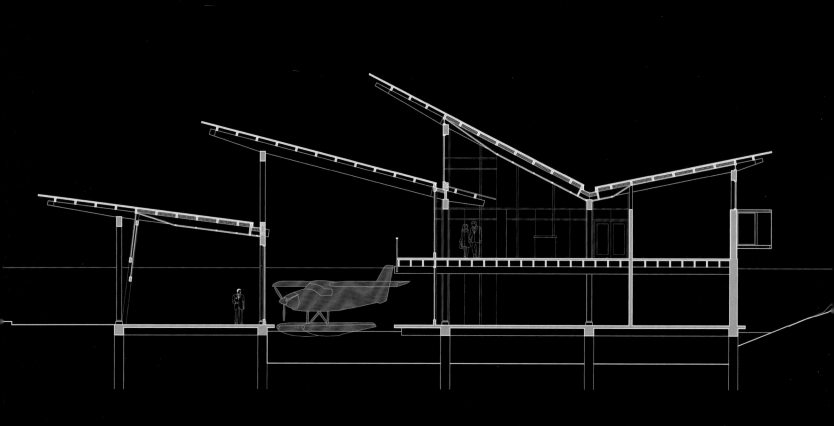

"For every compromise you knowingly make in your work,
the result represents your next client."

Rebecca Roberts, 2006

Left | Building Section

'Look son, now that you are going into practice you must remember: you must start off the way you'd like to finish.' Very important statement. That's the first thing to a young architect: start off the way you'd like to finish.

The other one he said, 'For every compromise you knowingly make in your work, the result represents your next client.' There's a truism for you. So the work begets the work. And that's really important I think.

Another thing I said a little earlier is, 'never be in a rush to be a success.' And I think that's very important. One of the things that I think is a real problem, I think, today is that people want to be on top of the pile by the time they're thirty.

1:04:58

You've got to want to be good. As Mies would have said, 'I'm not interested in being interesting; I'm only interested in being good.' And I think that's another truism. Just be interested in being good.

1:06:12

I used to be in competitive swimming and my father was working as our trainer for my brothers and sisters and me. We'd do our half, (in your terms half-mile swim) approximately five hundred meters, half a kilometer, and at the end of it he'd say (each afternoon after school in summer, we'd do this, and we'd do the same thing in the morning), 'You have to do a hundred meter swim breadth in a minute.' And we accepted that, but every now and again he used to say, 'I want you to do another hundred

41

Kozo Nozawa, 2006

Left | Tectonic Model

Above | Building Model

meters now, and I want you to break it even more. I want a fifty eight out of you per hundred meters.' And we'd say to him, 'You rotten son-of-a-bitch.'

[laughter]

And it wasn't till he explained after about a year to us, he said you know, 'In life, you think you're finished, you're exhausted, you've just got there, you've totally had enough, can't do another thing, and somebody'll come on you and say they want this done, or they want that done, or want something else done. And want you have to perform again.'

He said, 'You're the kid, I'm teaching you that you're going to have the extra energy to go that distance further.' And I think that's another bit of advice is: Don't give up; there's always extra energy that you have. There's always the ability to think and rethink.

End

A CONVERSATION BETWEEN FRIENDS

Glenn Murcutt + Juhani Pallasmaa
CAUP UW Lecture Series
April 11, 2008
Moderated by Peter Cohan

Monica Willemsen, 2006

Left | Tectonic Model

Peter Cohan: I was thinking about this, and I believe that Glenn may have won more awards than the number of buildings he has built. One of those awards is the Alvar Aalto Medal, which he won in 1992. At the ceremony in Helsinki he met our other distinguished speaker tonight, Juhani Pallasmaa. In the years that followed Glenn and Juhani have become very close friends, so I'm hoping that tonight we will just be able to eavesdrop on a remarkable conversation between two friends. So I would like to invite Glenn and Juhani to the table.

PC: I'd like to begin with a question about memories. Many architects can trace their interest in architecture to an early childhood memory. One of the most famous examples is Alvar Aalto's memory of playing under the big white table that his father used as a land surveyor. What memories do you have from your youth that might have foretold of a life devoted to architecture?

Glenn Murcutt: Well, not only was I born on the run, I lived in Papua New Guinea until I was six years of age when the Pacific War reached our area, and we left on a scorched earth policy. I can say that living in the region where I lived was one of the most profound experiences a child could have, raised by the Papua New Guineans, my language was Pidgin English as a first language. We lived in the region of the country where there was the practice a certain level of cannibalism and Europeans were a favorite fair. They would come down just before dusk and out of the hills above a creek called Surprise Creek, surprise indeed it was. You would see the Kunai grass, which has 1.5 meters tall, in your

Continued on page 49

PILCHUCK GLASS SCHOOL

Stanwood, Washington
Glenn Murcutt + Jim Nicholls | 2007

CLASS LIST - Adam Amsel, Anisa Baldwin Metzgar, Casey Borgen, Michael Bullman, Scott Crawford, Maria D'ambrosio, Jamie Geringer, Gifty John, Nathan Lambdin, Amanda Lewkowicz

The Pilchuck Glass School needs additional faculty and staff housing on their rural campus.

Located on a west-facing slope, overlooking the Puget Sound, the school's land shifts between forest and meadow. The campus is near Stanwood, about one hour north of Seattle.

The Glass School was founded in the early Seventies by Dale Chihuly, James Carpenter, Buster Simpson, and John and Anne Hauberg. The 'campus as camp' has a lodge, hot shops, studios, and artists-in-residence facilities, designed and built by both artists and architects.

The studio made two trips to the site at Pilchuck, the first to survey it and create a contoured site plan, and the second to stake out our building footprints.

PROGRAM

9 Sleeping Rooms Including: Sink, Writing Desk, Dresser Drawers, Coat Hooks, Ability to be Single or Double Occupancy, All Furniture Included, All Lighting Included, Cross Ventilation

Porch Area: Insect Screened

Communal Area: Galley Kitchen, Sitting, Washer and Dryer

2 Showers and Wash Closets

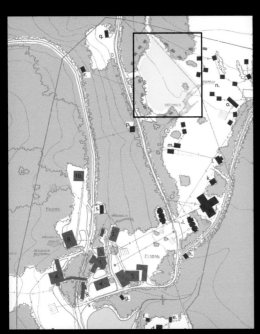

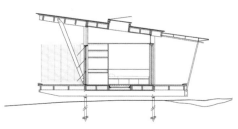

Scott Crawford, 2007

Left | Site Plan

Above Left | Tectonic Model

Above Right | Building Section

language that is 5 feet, and I can say they were 1.49 meters high. You would see this snake developing in the landscape, and an extraordinary fear would develop because you knew you would have to take the upper hand very quickly. The chief would come up to you, to my father in particular, and ask to sit down. The next thing, an axe would come out and… gone. Fortunately, my father was the leading south paw boxer in Sydney before he went, and he was just on 1.8m tall, compared with 1.49m, with a good long reach from the south paw, left leading. With a straight left lead, and a handful of pepper he was then King. Knocked the guy over. It was a terrible situation, but it was one of those things that you realized, you had to observe, you had to smell, you had to look, and you had to listen. You could smell from the winds, of the people getting closer, and you could hear the rustling in the grass and you observed this. This whole question of observation has been critical, absolutely critical to my life, to be able to read the country, to read the land, to read the water, to read the landscape.

This fear engendered in us was so powerful, and yet we had a very strong connection to Australia because each week the Gypsy Moth, this biplane, a single engine biplane, a pilot and a co-pilot in back, would fly over our property and around about 60 meters above the ground, just under 200 feet, the plane would do a right bank over our house and throw out our mail, so we had genuine air mail delivery.

And in the Kunai grass would land the bag with this huge tail, it was extraordinary. My final big memory was flight. The ability to lift off the ground and see planning strategies of villages was so

beautiful and it took me a long time to realize that these were villages as opposed to models because they looked like models to me as a very young child.

These were very vivid memories, and coming from that to Sydney, in a period of war, down to a street where the postman came with a whistle and dogs would bark and bite the postman, to the Catholic church which was nearby, with the nuns outside digging with forks and things, the fear of all this new world was amazing, but the critical thing was observation. The realization that you observe to be able to draw information of your particular environment was critical to my survival.

Juhani Pallasmaa: My childhood memories are not quite as exotic but they are equally profound. As Peter said, we are of the same age, so when I was three years old the Winter War broke out in Finland, and my mother took my five sisters and me to my grandfather's farm, and that tiny farm house in central Finland became my first and foremost university. In those days in the 30's and 40's a farmer had to know a thousand jobs. My grandfather could cure man and animal. He could build furniture, and all the objects needed in daily life. He could kill a bear or a moose. My grandmother could grow linen and make clothes. There were only two specialists in the entire village, the blacksmith and the priest. Otherwise, everybody did everything. I think it is this setting that made me open my eyes, and to be interested in all kinds of things. I know that some of my friends consider me over ambitious because I do all kinds of things. I don't think it is at all a matter of ambition, it is just reflecting this farmer background that everything is the same, that you can do everything in life, the main thing is that you do it as well as you can. Another thing that I would like to tell the young people here in the audience is that in those days in the forties, in a poor farmer family, there was only one book, the bible. There was no television, not even a radio. My great enchantment was a sample book of wallpapers, wallpaper models, that was my only visual stimulus, besides fighting my boredom by watching my grandfather do these fabulous things that he could do and then watching animals. I would want to say that boredom is an important aspect of growth, that it is actually the moment that a young child begins to develop his or her creative skills. Today's world goes 100% wrong educationally by trying to over stimulate the child… no… the child needs to be bored.

PC: …I thought it might be good to ask you to discuss your ideas about teaching and perhaps some of the lessons you are trying to convey…

Adam Amsel, 2007

Left | Exterior Porch Rendering

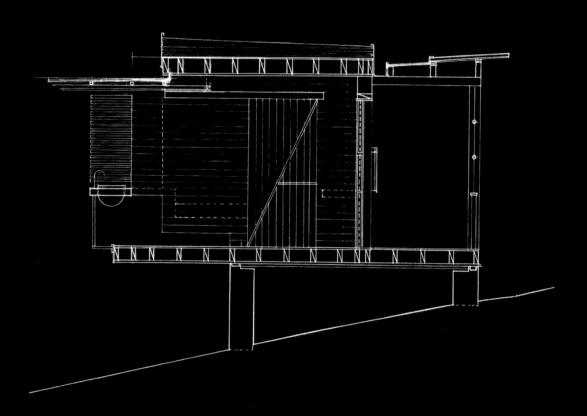

JP: Well, I must say sincerely that I don't pretend that I can teach architecture to anyone. I can perhaps provide an example of how to be an architect, what interests one might have, how to behave responsibly as an architect. Beyond that, my interest as a teacher is solely focused on the individuality of each student. For our educational systems anywhere in the western world, go forcefully against individuality, and an individual sense of responsibility. We are taught to believe in authority, and we are also taught always that there are wrong answers and right answers. In the artistic field there is no such categorization, wrong and right, it is only a qualitative difference. So for me, the greatest challenge is somehow to try to evoke the student's individuality, to make the student recognize his or her own persona, with all the limitations perhaps, and then, to make the student realize that he or she is eventually the final authority of the work. It is no use asking for an opinion of an external authority. My experience is that in today's architectural world, problems are so complex, particularly the legal aspects added to [them], that the architect does not have a chance to express or involve much off his emotions. So, in the studio the particular task that I am giving, [A setting for the Last Supper] takes away all these logistical difficulties from the problem, by using a ready-made room. You can't get anywhere with your logic when thinking about the Last Supper, and yet it is a function, so there is a functionalized exercise.

GM: I have always been interested in teaching in a way that clearly suppresses ego of the expressionist type, to the ego that is the driving force… I think the ego, as a driving force is very important. I was raised on Henry David Thoreau… "since most of us are going to be doing ordinary things in our lives, the most important thing about doing those ordinary things, is to do them extraordinarily well." That is extremely important to me. My father added, he said "and to be able to go to the beach where nobody knows who you are." Now that is not a very "starchitects" approach. It was a way of allowing you to become an individual without being arrogant, aggressive, and self-promoting. Most of us in my country would prefer to hide from a talk like this, or even any presentation. If somebody gave me the real opportunity by saying, "look, you don't have to do it," I'd take it. Because I operated alone for so long, I was under the woodwork for most of the time until this guy found me in 1992. Very little was known about anything I was doing, and the Finns with the Aalto medal are looking for someone who is unknown, and they go and expose you, and your finished.

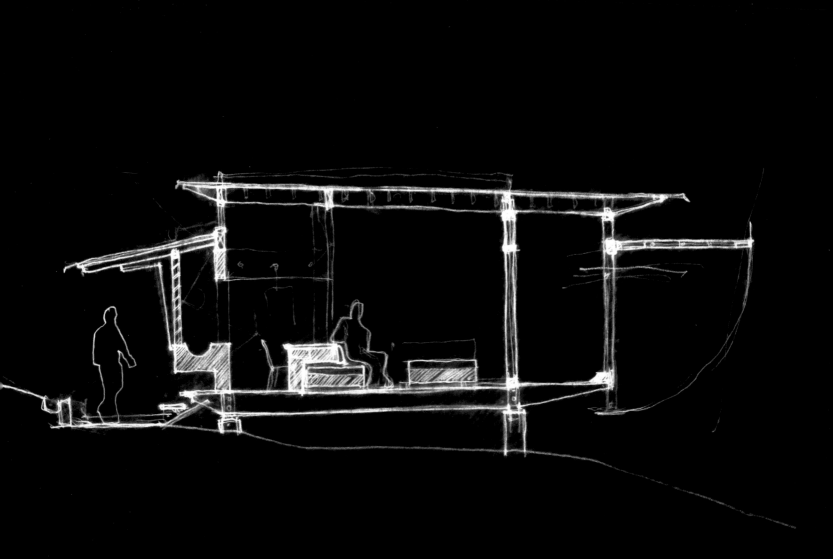

"I am interested in the local. It is very important to me to try and read the site."

My method of teaching, the way that I teach, is to try to bring out of your programs each of your personalities but to sometimes put ideas in front of you that will unlock a way of thinking, and that is very important to me. Juhani, you're right in saying that everybody, in teaching, really has to be taught individually. C.P. Vernon wrote a book called "Creativity" and describes two types of education, one is education for convergence, the other one is for divergence. Our education is largely based on convergence issues because it is easy to assess. There is an answer to a given question, but now, there are so many questions in life that simply do not have a given answer. The divergent process is what we are about, what art is about. What are the possibilities? How many possibilities are there? How does the site direct what we should be going? What is the responsibility to the site? Can we change elements of the site and still be responsible? Where does the wind come from? Where does the snow come from? What is the weather in summer? What is the change of seasons? When is the sun at a particular time of the year? What is the relationship of the sun and moisture, of the humidity factor? How does that relate to the building? Does the building need to be ventilated, or do you simply bludgeon it into what ever you want it to be, and put the air conditioning on? The answer is no. However, I see most places, the answer is yes. And so I'm very interested in understanding the local situation. Even though it is about a global thing, I am interested in the local. It is very important to me to try and read the site. If you design a project in the North Cascades, will the project be the same as it is in Florida? Well, I can I tell you, in most cases, in most parts of the world, pretty well yes.

"They are really important issues, and so the program we are running is very much about an ethical approach."

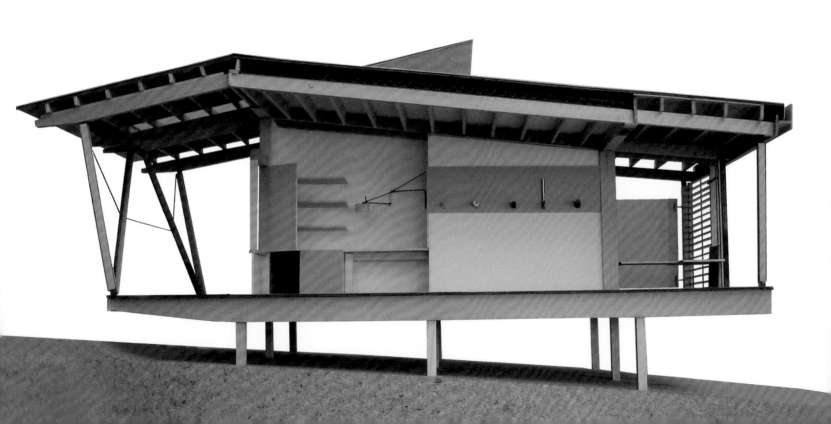

Nathan Lambdin, 2007

Left | Tectonic Model

You pump heating in, or you pump cooling in and you can do anything you like. I am not interested in that, and I think frankly it is an aspect of our profession that is unethical. I think that we must start to work ethically. As Juhani says, he is doing all these other things, I am doing all these other things, it is the things that bind us, and we are into all sorts of things together. They are really important issues, and so the program we are running is very much about an ethical approach, a responsibility to the land, a responsibility to materials, and how we use them appropriately and ethically.

PC: It is remarkable that both your memories of travel have involved indigenous people. I happen to know that both of you have worked extensively with the indigenous peoples of your own countries, I'd like you to comment a bit on the work you have done with them and perhaps the future of these peoples in each situation.

JP: I have done work with the Sami Lapp people in Northern Finland who are actually the last remaining indigenous people in Europe, and the last remaining group of people in the world that herd wild animals. As it happened, the museum project that I was working on took eight years to get full funding, so I had eight years of time, meeting with these reindeer herders and traveling with them up in Lapland and finding out about their life, and now I am expanding the museum by almost 100%. I am also on the jury for the new Sami cultural center that will be announced as an international competition next week by the Finnish government, which shows that, although there are only 6000 Sami people in Finland, the government is taking their case very ethically now. Together with EU, it has become a very strong ethical concern to take care of minorities.

GM: I have to correct my friend Juhani in saying they are the last people that herd. The Australian Aboriginals on the north of Australia, who many of them have had very little contact with Europeans, still use firestick technology for herding kangaroos, bringing them together. Many of the four legged animals are still herded though this firestick technology, and the use of spears, and so it is quite interesting that at the most remote parts of the earth, there is still this activity taking place.

JP: Maybe the European anthropologists do not consider kangaroos and your animals as animals. (Laughter)

GM: No they only consider the people as slightly rustic, a little closer to the animal kingdom perhaps.

Continued on page 61

TULA YOUNG HASTINGS FARM

Pullman, Washington
Glenn Murcutt + Peter Cohan | 2008

CLASS LIST - Todd Coglon, Amin Gilani, Zac Jensen, Jake LaBarre, Mac Lanphere, Charla Lemoine, Jessica Miller, Will Payne, Anna Pepper, Roman Pohorecki, Carl Von Rueden, Ane Sønderaal Tolfsen

The Tula Young Hastings farm is located about five miles outside of Pullman, Washington. It lies in the heart of the Palouse, a region characterized by rolling hills created by deposits of glacial silt left behind from the last ice age. Washington State University's Knott Dairy Center proposes to substantially renovate and expand current operations. The primary focus of the Murcutt studio was the design of a heifer barn and its related facilities. While in Pullman, Glenn instigated a discussion about the importance of the ethical treatment of animals and the need for a research institution like WSU to lead the way in developing techniques that promote such practices. The result of this discussion led to a series of additional program requirements: Heifers would be allowed to have freer access to the pastures by providing more direct connections from the barns to the pastures. Stage 1 and 2 heifers would be allowed to have contact, but not to nurse, with their mothers, adding pens for 55 mother cows and stalls for their calves. Heifers would also be protected from the extremes of weather. This resulted in a strong focus upon ventilation strategies, but also the need to fully enclose the pens in the winter. Lastly, efforts would be made to keep the heifers as clean as possible with alternative manure collection systems.

PROGRAM

Heifer Pens (minimum numbers):

Series 1: 10 Heifer Calves Weighing 150-250 lbs.

Series 2: 45 Young Heifers Weighing 250-400 lbs.

Series 3: 90 Older Heifers Weighing 400-800 lbs.

Series 4: 90 Full Grown Heifers Weighing 800-1200 lbs.

Main Barn: Veterinary Room, Scales Facility, Feed Room, Grain Bins, Hay Storage, Equipment Room, Locker Rooms with Bathrooms (Male & Female), Offices and a Classroom for 25 Students.

Optional Program Elements: Student Sleeping Quarters, Systems for Generating Energy Using Bio-Digesters and Methane Generators.

"The clarity of that light is amazing, to be able to get the ventilation at the same time, and the privacy at the same time, is a beautiful thing."

I have worked with aboriginal people, the power of mythology, their way of thinking, the beauty of their hierarchy. For example, you do not enter a building at right angles to the building. In the cave situation, with their beautiful paintings of hundreds of years and up to thousands of years ago, you enter from one end, and there is generally a guardian spirit and you ask of the guardian spirit permission to enter, and that is very important, you would never come up and enter the center, there is not that formality of the axis, it's always a side entry. That has been powerfully influential in my architecture. If you think, some of you would know the Simpson-Lee House, there are many other buildings that you enter from the edge, and this is an aboriginal notion. The parents sleep to the west of the children, the west is the end of the day, it's the sinking sun and it's the nearer to death, the morning is the east, is the beginning of the day, it's the future. This is really important to aboriginal people.

To actually have an ability to look out and to see who is coming, who is going, what weather pattern changes, what animals are moving on the horizon, is absolutely important. And, at the same time, not to be seen by people outside walking past during the day, to develop systems by which and through which one can mediate the internal environment to the prospect, to the view, and to be able at the same time to be able to work with the climate and to be able to get ventilation, to be able to get the low level of light, because the light is so clear. The clarity of that light is amazing, to be able to get the ventilation at the same time, and the privacy at the same time, is a beautiful thing. So working with aboriginal people from the level of planning strategies, of where children sleep, where

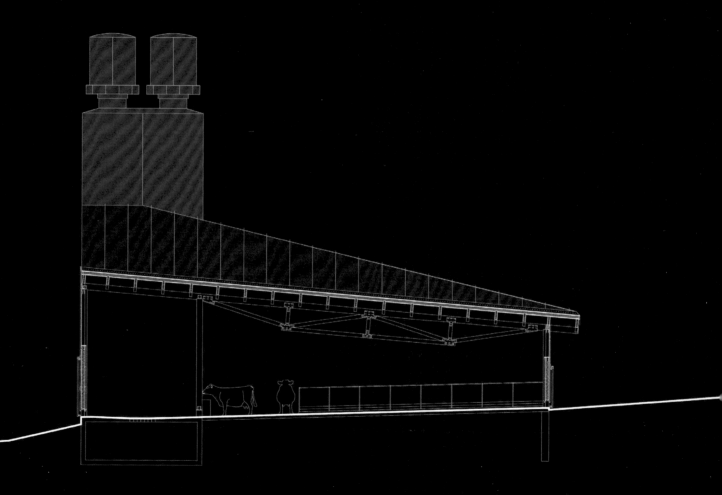

"They haven't survived through the fittest; it's an entirely different process to survival through cooperation."

the mother sleeps, the father sleeps, where the grandchildren sleep. There are whole different cultural requirements, and it is upon us as Europeans to understand this. The aboriginal people have worked with the land and they survive through cooperation. They haven't survived through the fittest; it's an entirely different process to survive through cooperation. The longest living single culture in the world has been survival through cooperation.

JP: Let me just add one thing. In designing for indigenous cultures like the case of this Sami Lapp museum, there is a special responsibility because for instance, among the Sami people, who were nomadic peoples moving along with their reindeer herds, there was never a cultural institution ever in their life, so there is no traditional model for a museum, yet it has to be somehow fixed, the imagery of that place and that culture, so an architect faces an almost impossible task to invent a tradition that never existed, and still has to be true.

PC: Juhani and Glenn you seem to have worked primarily in your own countries so I wonder if you would care to comment on the whole trend in architecture now towards a global practice?

GM: Well, as you know I have not built a single project outside the borders of my land, and will not be building a single project outside the borders of my land. My country extends the size of the United States of America, I go from the monsoon tropics, the wet tropics, the warm temperate, the temperate, the cool temperate the hot arid, the coastal, the 1000 to 3000 meter high, we have so many climates in Australia that the extensive nature of the land provides more than necessary enough places to build.

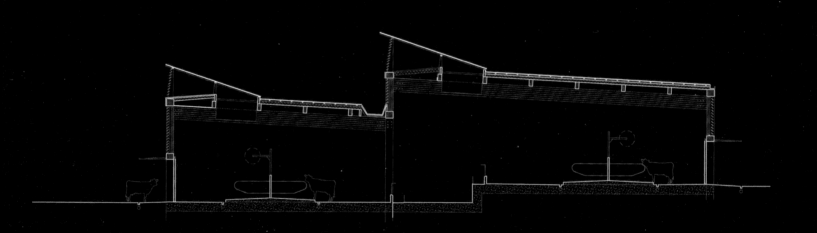

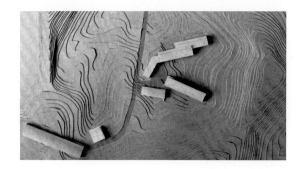

Ane Sønderaal Tolfsen, 2008

Left | Building Section

Above | Site Model

I don't need to go on to the trees of the world to leave my mark as dogs do. It is totally unnecessary for me to do that. That doesn't deny that there may be some projects worth doing outside of one's country, but I sometimes feel that it is more important for many of us to build all over the planet. To have the same building, the same looking building, and you just pump more cold air in, or more hot air in, this does not understand the planet. For me the most important thing is understanding place, understanding culture, understanding technology, and that in your own place is really complicated. To understand your own culture takes a lifetime. To understand somebody else's culture will probably take two or three lifetimes. And it is so easy to make terrible mistakes. I think we are going to start seeing a retraction of what we have been blowing all over the world, like the wind takes the seed to everywhere. I don't need to do that. If one doesn't need to, then why should one ever do it? I find that working with my own culture, with my own place, is really important.

To understand the nature of materials, that a brick or a stone is a compressive material, and to put it in an arch, to put it in a span, you've got to go into compression. To understand steel is extremely good in tension, but very poor in compression, to actually put a very thin piece of steel between two cheeks of very good timber, you can get some very nice spans out of composite construction. To understand where materials come from, to understand that timber takes 5 mega-joules a kilogram to process from the forest, that to understand that the tree, in the first 20 years of its life, is going to take in carbon dioxide and all the carbons, and be able to give back oxygen, while after 20 years it is pretty

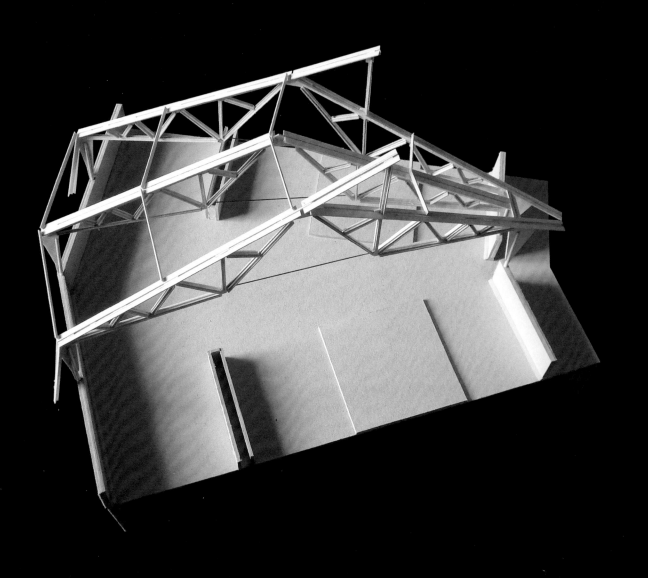

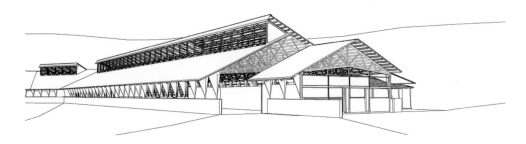

William G. Payne III, 2008

Left | Tectonic Model

Above | Building Perspective

stable. To understand that steel takes 40 mega-joules per kilogram to process, to understand that lime for cement takes 2 per kilogram, to understand that aluminum takes 143 mega-joules. This teaches us how much of these products we should perhaps not be using or how much we should be using. Certain materials, in the energy, in the gaining of it all, are so, so destructive. We have got to be very responsible. You simply don't think of a brick as being a piece of material that you put on a building. The brick comes from somewhere; these beautiful things are destroying other places. So, I have become somewhat interested in the process of building, I am interested in the way you put buildings together, so that they can be pulled apart very easily and the materials reused so that recycling is extremely important in the way we design. We know that all buildings are going to change in their production, they are going to change in their planning, and so if we can reuse materials, to move them about is important. So the idea of globalization has limited appeal to me, but the principles are transferable. If you ask the right questions of any place you can probably get an appropriate answer. But, the cultural issues are the tricky ones. Over to you, Juhani.

JP: I am equally critical about the process of globalization. It is primarily an economic enterprise, and of course supported by technology, that tends towards universality and communications. As Glenn said, culture can hardly be learned, culture needs to be lived. Consequently, it is not possible at all, on a very fundamental level, to build on different cultural grounds, simply because you do not understand the historical layered unconscious levels of cultures. It usually becomes a cartoon, or just takes place

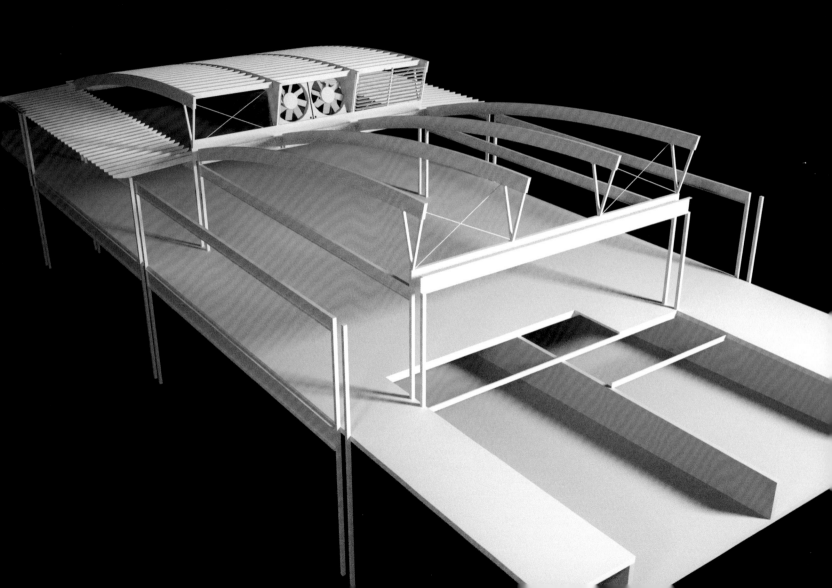

on this singular level of globalized style. I think this is a very unfortunate phase in architecture, that our craft is seen as a universally applicable exercise. I am also rather critical myself about a business attitude in architecture. I think architecture is primarily grounded on human and cultural ground. I have never seen my personal work or interests along those lines. I think it is exactly this attitude, of seeing architecture primarily as a business, which has given so much power to globalization. I am currently renovating the Finnish embassy in Beijing, so I have been going back and forth, so I have seen the tragedy of China. Beijing, one of the finest cities and finest cultures on earth has become, I would use the word vandalized, by international architecture. Beijing is the most dreadful place. For me, it is really a vision of the gloomy future of mankind if we don't come to our senses.

End of Conversation

Mac Lamphere, 2008

Left | Tectonic Model

JUROR'S COMMENT

Carlos Jimenez
Professor, Rice School of Architecture
Principal, Carlos Jimenez Studio

Final review panel for Murcutt Studio 2007

Photo: John Stamets

During my delightful afternoon as a juror in Glenn Murcutt's studio at U of W, I was able to observe the subtle and precise elevation of local conditions to universal insights (and vice-versa). To experience the breath of this transformation across the work of the students was a true delight, as it was to view Murcutt's patient and generous gifts as teacher and critic. I marveled at the reciprocal exchange of these gifts and understood then how privileged the students were. The inspiring and demanding tempo of the studio will remain one of the most valuable and memorable experiences for everyone involved, as it will be for the entire school.

Review Panels for Studio Final Reviews

2004	2005	2006	2007	2008
Bob Hull	Einar Jarmund	Jay Deguchi	Carlos Jiminez	Carlos Jiminez
Tom Kundig	Rahul Mehrota	Lisa Findley	Dave Miller	John Patkau
George Suyama		Susan Jones	Patrica Patkau	Patricia Patkau
		Tom Kundig	John Reed	Anthony Pellechia
		David Strauss		
		Gordon Walker		
		Ed Weinstein		

HOW GLENN CAME TO TEACH AT THE UNIVERSITY OF WASHINGTON

Dr. Vikramaditya Prakash
Professor

Glenn Murcutt opening the wall at the Simpson-Lee house. Photo: Rick Mohler

Why Glenn Murcutt? Why here at the University of Washington in Seattle?

One of the things that many of our faculty are committed to is the idea of Regionalism, the conviction that the core values that generate good architecture can be discovered through a profound understanding of the specificities of place. Issues of geography, climate, urban context, local materials, and local cultural expressions are often championed in our studios and seminar courses.

Yet the question could be asked: in a world that is becoming increasingly globalized, increasingly interconnected and inter-dependent, is not regionalism in danger of being marginalized? The unimagined transparency and immediacy created by the digital network have created a global situation in which people can collaborate from great distances, and on the more positive side, people spread throughout the world are more aware than ever of each, and each others lives and aspirations. At the same time, the US victory in the Cold War has resulted in the global domination of capitalist economies. Our anxieties now come from the horrors of a uniform carpet of McCulture spreading across the globe, modeled vapidly on American commercial culture. And yet, politically speaking, there is so much distrust in the world today, with destructive fictions such as 'clash of civilizations' routinely making the rounds of the talk shows. What we need is greater understanding of each other, accompanied with a conscious effort to appreciate and engage each other's civilization. We cannot remain caged within our own cultural cocoons. If there is one thing more dangerous than the spread of a global McCulture, then that would be the spread of a global McCocoon culture. Cocoons make war.

Recently, our department was also in the midst of one of those provost-mandated 'strategic planning' processes, when the discussion turned to question ethics of design in our studios, and, in that context, the role of small practices like Glenn's in the global economy. Several faculty noted that they had spent a fair amount of time trotting around the globe, interviewing and looking at the work of some of the smaller, more local, well-established, but not quite name-brand, architects practicing in various cities of the world. Good work, they argued, is a product of sensitive and sensible design values, and not always proportional to project cost. It can be found everywhere; no one country has a monopoly on it. Discussions amongst our faculty revealed that 'good architecture' in their opinion had to do with a common set of shared principles and affections for a particular approach to architectural design. It was connected with being small and specific, but not really regionalism. It is not a question of appearances. Sometimes things look similar, sometimes not. It is not a question of style. It is rather a question of a shared set of values of architectural design. Values are more important for the process of design, rather than the product.

From this came the concept of "Global Architecture/Local Architects" – the idea that there is a global network of local architects, who are linked together by a network architectural values. A decentered global movement, other than that of the global design firms practicing global, and the global 'star' architects, designing worldwide, a by-product of the global economy.

So, one can argue that there is a global network of local architects, and Glenn Murcutt is an important node in this network. And that is how Glenn Murcutt came to teach at UW.

End

Glenn Murcutt operating the Simpson-Lee house
Photo: Rick Mohler

Column and forest detail, Simpson-Lee house

Photo: Rick Mohler

THE MASTER CLASS

Dave Miller, FAIA
Chair, University of Washington
Department of Architecture

Intellectual exchange between educators and practitioners in the design studio environment is critical to architectural education at the University of Washington. Glenn Murcutt's work informs a theory of architecture shared by the academic culture at the UW Department of Architecture. These aligned principles mine the poetic potential of an architecture embedded in material construction and the power of place. The lessons of Glenn's master studio, taught collaboratively with a studio faculty member, reinforces a problem solving approach that goes beyond formal manipulation and pragmatic solution, advancing the craft of the detail and its integration with site, systems and structure. Respected by students, professionals and professors, Glenn Murcutt's architecture and teaching manifests a highly developed design philosophy.

Glenn Murcutt offers an exacting model of the truly ethical practice. Celebrated and awarded with international recognition, Glenn remains accessible and personally engaged with each student. He is an articulate instructor, with a wealth of personal examples and references to draw upon. His work has embodied the principles of sustainability before the movement had a label, each built project is deeply influenced by the land as a physical and cultural place. While encouraging design solutions that propose acts of restitution, Glenn develops a student's deep understanding of the latent forces of nature, where the site informs the building while the building tunes the human experience. He offers these lessons to the students with absolute clarity, consistency and conviction.

End

Jessica Miller + Glenn Murcutt in UW studio

Photo: Peter Cohan